PREPARING THE BODY

Preparing the Body

YesYes Books Portland

Norma
Liliana
Valdez

PREPARING THE BODY © 2019 BY NORMA LILIANA VALDEZ
FIRST EDITION

COVER ART © MARIA TOMASULA,
"WHAT THE WATER GAVE (FOR FRIDA)"
COVER & INTERIOR DESIGN: ALBAN FISCHER
PROJECT LEAD EDITOR: STEVIE EDWARDS

ISBN 978-1-936919-76-5
PRINTED IN THE UNITED STATES OF AMERICA

PUBLISHED BY YESYES BOOKS
1614 NE ALBERTA ST
PORTLAND, OR 97211
YESYESBOOKS.COM

KMA SULLIVAN, PUBLISHER
STEVIE EDWARDS, SENIOR EDITOR, BOOK DEVELOPMENT
ALBAN FISCHER, GRAPHIC DESIGNER
DEVI GONZALES, MANAGING EDITOR
COLE HILDEBRAND, SENIOR EDITOR OF OPERATIONS
LUTHER HUGHES, ASSISTANT EDITOR & YYB TWITTER
AMBER RAMBHAROSE, EDITOR, ART LIFE & INSTAGRAM
CARLY SCHWEPPE, ASSISTANT EDITOR, *VINYL*
ALEXIS SMITHERS, ASSISTANT EDITOR, *VINYL* & YYB FACEBOOK
PHILLIP B. WILLIAMS, COEDITOR IN CHIEF, *VINYL*
AMIE ZIMMERMAN, EVENTS COORDINATOR
HARI ZIYAD, ASSISTANT EDITOR, *VINYL*

*for my sisters
in blood and poetry*

God still owes me a drink for every time
the woman I should be has died.
—SARA BORJAS

Contents

[who hushed] — 1

How I Learned to Lie — 3

La Descarada — 4

Rue — 5

How to Search for Your Child — 6

Tepoztlán Blues — 7

Lobo — 8

Guitarist — 10

After Ocean — 11

What I Want for the Body — 13

You'll Be Given Love — 14

All I Want — 15

Saudade — 17

Preparing the Body — 18

Rupture — 19

Acknowledgments — 23
Notes — 27

who hushed
my legs
queried
my skirt
whose foul finger
whispered
your body
is not your own
who said
wither

How I Learned to Lie

The smell of smoke lodged in my nostrils, the wine-tart
of his mouth. The way his tongue rots every time he lies

only I know. I have been accomplice, have been culprit.
When he's not looking I rub my lips tight with a washcloth.

Gardenias must die here. I hide secrets in the dresser.
Stuff them so dust-deep you'll never find. All I wanted

was to wear my hair down. To feel something like wildfire.
Say it. Every day in this city there are quiet violations

we keep to ourselves. I've not known the full use of my body.
It's like the time I scrawled the wall raw with my fingernails.

What is left under my skin splinters.

La Descarada

My left leg dangles over the dresser. I am not wearing shoes, only underwear. I am disappearing into window and wall, head tossed back and faceless into plaster. My midriff in glass. My midriff could be glass. Beyond glass could be roofs. I'm disappearing onto roofs in another country; another country not of my choosing where blooms are, at closer look, mourning doves. Mourning doves cooing from little stomachs. Overstuffed little stomachs cooing nonetheless. Mourning doves rancid blooms in an overripe gardenia bush. Gardenias make my stomach queasy. Too many gardenias stuffed inside me. In my mouth his fist and the gardenias. His thumb buried inside my clavicle searching for the off button hidden somewhere beneath blooms and mourning.

Rue

wound

scar tissue and a mouth full of

landscape—

    unwed/bitter/bruise

desert

of ruin:

    my fair linen, a crimson crêpe de Chine

    bloody dress cut to pieces

no altar for this—

    no baptismal gown

    no offering of baby's

    breath

    no roses

How to Search for Your Child

Colinas de Santa Fe, Veracruz, México

Drive a six-foot metal rod into ground.
With each click-clack of hammer
dig the cross-shaped bar deeper into soil.
Pull out the rod.
Bring it close to your nose.
Inhale. Wet earth or remains?
Exhume 253 bodies, none of them yours.
Yellow your skin.
Grow your hair waist-length.

Tepoztlán Blues

Orchids hang from the patio ceiling.
When no one is watching
I will take one and put it in my pocket
as if I could own something of this place.
By morning, it will be dead. I'll walk by a funeral
home with child-sized caskets, and cry.
The air will belong to firewood. Night will return
cold to my bones. I'll be alebrije: half woman
half moon. On the feast of San Sebastián
fireworks rise and fall, like us all.
Orchestras will be spark then ash.
Nothing here is tame. I am high and disoriented
pulled by my entrails. I'll dance mezcal blues.
His hand inside my thigh will be a hovering question:
How can we do this, and where?
It won't be enough for the way I want
to swallow this country: whole.

Lobo

I was already gutted when you found me in full-
moon's eve. I was already split and cavity.

My face, a calavera: eye sockets and mandible
cheek bones. My teeth exposed to the wisdoms.

I'd been drinking blues from what I hoped would be
a bottomless night. You approached with slackened ears

sniffed with wetted nose. You kept your canines
to yourself. I bore my bony fingers into pelt, hushed

and rough, and soothed the patches at your nape.
Your eyes slit-like then. What I remember most:

the obsidian in your gaze, sharper than a razor.
How you finished off the gutting like a cool stream of river.

How I began to flesh. Shape-shifter,
I've yet to hear the low pitch of your howl.

We were on a street called Jacarandas.
In the dead of winter I've forgotten how to name blossoms.

Guitarist

On a gravel-dusted floor
I danced alone. My hips honey
loosened by his Strat.
The lead singer moaned shotgun
loaded to the sky, or the devil inside.
I couldn't understand a word. But night
was not about words. All that mattered
was the howling of my insides
the brief glorious fire
of his hands.

After Ocean

& this is how we danced: shadows lifted
from the streets, late February turning our hunger

into plums, ripe in our palms. The cempazúchitl
veils of gold. Your whisper lulled night

through my hair—my hair a river's current. We spelled
our names in heartbeats and spilled ourselves

like bracken waters. When our lips did not touch
the moon broke like rain clouds. In echoes of her thunder

splintered bones, limbs disjointed. *The body's inevitable
unraveling.* Beneath our feet

splitting stones and another cumbia, another current.
Waxing. Waning. Time stood useless

motionless to our farewell. Which is to say: I found breath in you. Which is to say:

The cenzontle's song had already left its body.

What I Want for the Body

nereidas at dusk
open-air
   dancehall
       at the small of the back
      trumpets/trombones/timbales

rivulets of sweat and
your hand

your chest to dwell
in

fishnets

calf's-length of chiffon
      to exit the night

a name for me in náhuatl

You'll Be Given Love

The first movement was this: her touch
in the softness of my hair.

My hair giving over to the wilderness under
her sun. All day it blew surrendered in its gestures.

Her hands startled me a little
enough to shake the blackbird in my cage.

That guardian of never-would-be's
even he rattled

fell off his perch
and turned to humming.

All I Want

   All I want is my lover's breath
at my nape
  his arms—
    vines of blooming
petals
  'round my hips.
    Not this red-
pooled mourning.
    Not this crimson spilt.
  I wake
and he is
   ghost-gone. Taken
by the trigger.
    I dream his blurred and honey-
  suckled fingers settling on my waist
a trip wire:
     all about to spark
  cicadas/lilies/white gloves.

What am I to do

with the burning?

    With the rage between

        prayer and throat?

My tongue detonates.

        The bullets now my teeth.

Saudade

My body sung blue
        sung soft
My body sung
        blue note
Sung winter
        torn nights
How to sleep
        this bed
Each note
        sung sad
Sung bone deep
My body sung
        blue soft
My body sung blue
        sung soft
My body sung
        undone

Preparing the Body

Fine scissor to little-girl-like.
Inspect for gray. Remove by tweezing.
Razor to upper thigh's edge.
Stand in mirror and say *no*, say *too late*, say *lonely*.
Say *forget it*, and *who anyway*.
Close all the doors. Put on the mother mask
the ill-fitting wife mask, and go make dinner.
The flesh you'll cut into is already dead.
You'll hate yourself for it.

Rupture

I am the breast I hold
in each hand
Each breast my breast
small as they be
mine nonetheless
I say *never*
I say *no one*
Say *when was the last time I*
My mascara a night old
I wake on Friday and ask
What is this body anyway
Morgan answers
The body
is a person
is a person
is a person
The body is a person
This body is not a fucking abstraction
When was the last time

is a question I ask too much
Instead I should ask
When will be the next time
or *the first time I*
check myself
I check myself
into a hotel
Begin like this: cheap brut and a buzz
I want a buzz in my muscle
a buckle in my memory
a stumble
I want a stumble and something electric
something historic and undead
Undead for god's sake
something undead and a current
inside me
I send a friend a text
of my moodiness
There is no bathtub for my glass
for everything that's fracturing
because everything is indeed fracturing
the hours

our touching

the letters in my name

I want the crumble

I say bring on

the crumble

the crooked stumble

bring on the rupture

Acknowledgments

Many thanks to the editors of the following journals in which poems in this chapbook first appeared, especially Adriana E. Ramírez, Angie Cruz, Jenn Givhan, and Blas Falconer.

Huizache Magazine: "How I Learned to Lie"

Aster(ix) Journal: "How to Search for Your Child" and "After Ocean"

Tinderbox Poetry Journal: "Tepoztlán Blues" and "Lobo"

The Los Angeles Review: "You'll Be Given Love"

Ursa Minor: "Saudade"

Mil gracias to companions on this poetic journey. Kenneth Chacon for seeing the poet in me before I recognized her. Daniel Vazquez, founder and president of the fan club. Xingona Collective comadres Leticia Del Toro, Aida Salazar, Yaccaira

Salvatierra, and Suzy Huerta Quezada for the shared joys and challenges of this woman/artist/mother life. Joseph Rios for late night oldies. Sara Borjas for writing words I couldn't. Sivan Rotholz Teitelman for seeing me in that first ever poetry workshop. Dickson Lam for uplifting me as a writer and for complicity in all things social justice at CCC. MK Chavez for unconditional belief in my poems. Kristina Bicher for reading first drafts with care and understanding. Maritza Jackson Sandoval and Benjamin Figueroa for the sanctuary of friendship.

To the writing communities that have nurtured me: Macondo, CantoMundo, VONA, Círculo de Poetas, Community of Writers, Hedgebrook. With special gratitude to Under the Volcano International and Magda Bogin, for showing me home to Tepoztlán. Reyna Grande for first inviting me. Mil gracias Tonatiuh Rodriguez Quiroz, hermano del alma, por abrirme las puertas de ese pueblo mágico tan tuyo. Gracias Micaela Sánchez Miranda por ese rinconcito al pie de cerros donde nacieron algunos de estos poemas.

To the many teachers who have taught me the delicate joy of reading, writing, and revising especially Laura Walker and

Sherwin Bitsui. To my editor, Stevie Edwards, who read every word of this manuscript with precise attention. To KMA Sullivan, Jill Kolongowski, and everyone at YesYes Books for bringing this book to life. Maria Tomasula for gracing these poems with such gorgeous artwork and Francisco Aragón for making this possible.

All my love and gratitude to my family. My most precious hearts, Sebastian and Alejandro Jimenez. Javier (Chino) Jimenez, my partner in bringing these boys into the world and raising them with all our love. My parents Maria de los Angeles and Juvenal Valdez. My sister Cecilia Valdez for the countless hours you cared for my sons so that I could write. My sisters Rosa Maria Valdez and Susie Valdez for teaching me the artist's way. Ana Portnoy Brimmer and Salima Hamirani for all the ways you've taught me love. Suzy Huerta Quezada for eternal sisterhood in all things life and poetry. Por vida, hermanas, por vida.

Notes

The epigraph by Sara Borjas is from her poem "A Heart Can Be Broken Only Once, Like a Window."

"How I Learned to Lie" is written after Javier Zamora's poem, "How I Learned to Walk."

"La Descarada" is an ekphrastic poem based on a painting of the same name by the Mexican artist, Rafael Cauduro.

"How to Search for Your Child" describes the method used by El Colectivo Solecito, a group of mothers in Veracruz, who search for their disappeared children, victims of the narco war in Mexico.

"After Ocean" borrows language from, and engages some syntactical mirroring in Ocean Vuong's poem "Homewrecker." The line, "The body's inevitable unraveling," is a direct quote taken from Lee Ann Roripaugh's blurb of Vuong's chapbook *NO* (YesYes Books, 2013).

"You'll Be Given Love" takes as its title the first lyric from the song "All is Full of Love" by Björk.

"All I Want" is dedicated to Diamond Reynolds and Salena Manni, partners of Philando Castile and Stephon Clark.

"Rupture" references Morgan Parker's poem "Magical Negro #84: The Black Body."

NORMA LILIANA VALDEZ is a member of the Macondo Writers Workshop and a CantoMundo fellow. Her work appears in *The Rumpus, The Los Angeles Review, Tinderbox Poetry Journal*, and the anthology *Latinas: Struggles & Protests in 21st Century USA*, among others. Norma earned a BA in Psychology, an MS in Counseling, and a graduate certificate in Ethnic Studies from San Francisco State University. She is an alumna of the UC Berkeley Extension Writing Program and has been awarded residencies and fellowships from Hedgebrook, Under the Volcano International, Community of Writers, and VONA, in addition to others. She is a founding member of the Xingona Collective, a women's writing group whose mission is to nurture a sustaining writing practice for its members through mutual encouragement and writing retreats. She lives in the Bay Area.

Also from YesYes Books

FULL-LENGTH COLLECTIONS

Ugly Music by Diannely Antigua

i be, but i ain't by Aziza Barnes

The Feeder by Jennifer Jackson Berry

Gutter by Lauren Brazeal

What Runs Over by Kayleb Rae Candrilli

This, Sisyphus by Brandon Courtney

Blues Triumphant by Jonterri Gadson

Ceremony of Sand by Rodney Gomez

Undoll by Tanya Grae

Everything Breaking/For Good by Matt Hart

Sons of Achilles by Nabila Lovelace

Reaper's Milonga by Lucian Mattison

Landscape with Sex and Violence by Lynn Melnick

GOOD MORNING AMERICA I AM HUNGRY AND ON FIRE
    by jamie mortara

Stay by Tanya Olson

a falling knife has no handle by Emily O'Neill

I'm So Fine: A List of Famous Men & What I Had On by Khadijah Queen

If the Future Is a Fetish by Sarah Sgro

Gilt by Raena Shirali

[insert] boy by Danez Smith

CHAPBOOK COLLECTIONS

Vinyl 45s

After by Fatimah Asghar

Inside My Electric City by Caylin Capra-Thomas

Dream with a Glass Chamber by Aricka Foreman

Exit Pastoral by Aidan Forster

Of Darkness and Tumbling by Mónica Gomery

Makeshift Cathedral by Peter LaBerge

A History of Flamboyance by Justin Phillip Reed

Unmonstrous by John Allen Taylor

Giantess by Emily Vizzo

No by Ocean Vuong

This American Ghost by Michael Wasson

Blue Note Editions

Beastgirl & Other Origin Myths by Elizabeth Acevedo

Kissing Caskets by Mahogany L. Browne

One Above One Below: Positions & Lamentations by Gala Mukomolova

Companion Series

Inadequate Grave by Brandon Courtney

The Rest of the Body by Jay Deshpande